Article 8

The Right to Preservation of Identity

Article 9

The Right Not to Be Separated from
His or Her Parents

A Commentary on the United Nations Convention
on the Rights of the Child

Editors

André Alen, Johan Vande Lanotte, Eugeen Verhellen,
Fiona Ang, Eva Berghmans and Mieke Verheyde

Article 8

The Right to Preservation of Identity

Article 9

The Right Not to Be Separated from His or Her Parents

By

Jaap E. Doek

Chairperson of the UN Committee on the Rights of the Child.
Professor of Law at the Free University of Amsterdam

MARTINUS NIJHOFF PUBLISHERS
LEIDEN • BOSTON
2006

This book is printed on acid-free paper.

A Cataloging-in-Publication record for this book is available from the Library of Congress.

Cite as: J.E. Doek, "Article 8: The Right to Preservation of Identity, and Article 9: The Right Not to Be Separated from His or Her Parents", in: A. Alen, J. Vande Lanotte, E. Verhellen, F. Ang, E. Berghmans and M. Verheyde (Eds.) *A Commentary on the United Nations Convention on the Rights of the Child* (Martinus Nijhoff Publishers, Leiden, 2006).

ISSN 1574-8626
ISBN-13: 978-90-04-14864-2
ISBN-10: 90-04-14864-7

© 2006 by Koninklijke Brill NV, Leiden, The Netherlands.
Koninklijke Brill NV incorporates the imprints Brill Academic Publishers, Martinus Nijhoff Publishers and VSP.

Cover image by Nadia, 1 $^1/_2$ years old.

http://www.brill.nl

PRINTED IN THE NETHERLANDS

CONTENTS

LIST OF ABBREVIATIONS

African Charter	African Charter on the Rights and Welfare of the Child
CCPR	International Covenant on Civil and Political Rights
CRC	International Convention on the Rights of the Child
CRC Committee	UN Committee on the Rights of the Child
ECHR	European Convention on Human Rights
ECtHR	European Court of Human Rights
UN	United Nations

AUTHOR BIOGRAPHY

Jaap E. Doek is Emeritus Professor of Law (Family and Juvenile Law) at the Vrije Universiteit of Amsterdam (since July 2004). He has been the Dean of the Law Faculty at the Vrije Universiteit (1988–1992). From 1998–2003 he was an Extraordinary Professor of Juvenile Law at the University of Leiden. Currently he is a Deputy Justice in the Court of Appeal of Amsterdam and he has been a juvenile court judge in the district court of Alkmaar and The Hague (1978–1985).

He is (since May 2001) the Chairperson of the UN Committee on the Rights of the Child.

Professor Doek has been a founding member of the International Society for the Prevention of Child Abuse and Neglect (ISPCAN) and board member 1976–1992 (President 1982–1984 and Vice-President for developing countries, 1984–1992) and in that capacity was involved in the establishment of the African Network for Prevention and Protection of Child Abuse and Neglect (ANPPCAN). He was also involved in the creation of Defence for Children International (DCI; 1979) and the Dutch Section of this organisation (1984). He has been a member of an ISPCAN/DCI working group on Child Labour which conducted a large study on Child Labour (1994–1997). He was a member of the Board of the International Association of Juvenile and Family Court Magistrates 1982–1986).

In 1993, he was a visiting scholar at Georgetown University Law School in Washington DC (February–July) and at Michigan University School of Law in Ann Arbor (September–December). In the Spring of 1999 (January–May) he was a visiting professor at the North Western University School of Law in Chicago. In 1999–2000 he was the President of the European Law Faculties Association (ELFA).

In February 1999 he was elected as a member (Rapporteur since May 1999), re-elected in February 2003, and Chairperson since May 2001 of the UN Committee on the Rights of the Child.

He has published numerous books and articles on various topics in the area of children's rights and family law in national (Dutch) and international (English) journals.

TEXT OF ARTICLE 8

ARTICLE 8

1. States Parties undertake to respect the right of the child to preserve his or her identity, including nationality, name and family relations as recognized by law without unlawful interference.

2. Where a child is illegally deprived of some or all of the elements of his or her identity, States Parties shall provide appropriate assistance and protection, with a view to speedily re-establishing his or her identity.

ARTICLE 8

1. Les Etats parties s'engagent à respecter le droit de l'enfant de préserver son identité, y compris sa nationalité, son nom et ses relations familiales, tels qu'ils sont reconnus par la loi, sans ingérence illégale.

2. Si un enfant est illégalement privé des éléments constitutifs de son identité ou de certains d'entre eux, les Etats parties doivent lui accorder une assistance et une protection appropriées, pour que son identité soit rétablie aussi rapidement que possible.

ARTICLE 9

1. States Parties shall ensure that a child shall not be separated from his or her parents against their will, except when competent authorities subject to judicial review determine, in accordance with applicable law and procedures, that such separation is necessary for the best interests of the child. Such determination may be necessary in a particular case such as one involving abuse or neglect of the child by the parents, or one where the parents are living separately and a decision must be made as to the child's place of residence.

2. In any proceedings pursuant to paragraph 1 of the present article, all interested parties shall be given an opportunity to participate in the proceedings and make their views known.

3. States Parties shall respect the right of the child who is separated from one or both parents to maintain personal relations and direct contact with both parents on a regular basis, except if it is contrary to the child's best interests.

ARTICLE 9

1. Les Etats parties veillent à ce que l'enfant ne soit pas séparé de ses parents contre leur gré, à moins que les autorités compétentes ne décident, sous réserve de révision judiciaire et conformément aux lois et procédures applicables, que cette séparation est nécessaire dans l'intérêt supérieur de l'enfant. Une décision en ce sens peut être nécessaire dans certains cas particuliers, par exemple lorsque les parents maltraitent ou négligent l'enfant, ou lorsqu'ils vivent séparément et qu'une décision doit être prise au sujet du lieu de résidence de l'enfant.

2. Dans tous les cas prévus au paragraphe 1 du présent article, toutes les parties intéressées doivent avoir la possibilité de participer aux délibérations et de faire connaître leurs vues.

3. Les Etats parties respectent le droit de l'enfant séparé de ses deux parents ou de l'un d'eux d'entretenir régulièrement des relations personnelles et des contacts directs avec ses deux parents, sauf si cela est contraire à l'intérêt supérieur de l'enfant.

4. Where such separation results from any action initiated by a State Party, such as the detention, imprisonment, exile, deportation or death (including death arising from any cause while the person is in the custody of the State) of one or both parents or of the child, that State Party shall, upon request, provide the parents, the child or, if appropriate, member of the family with the essential information concerning the whereabouts of the absent member(s) of the family unless the provision of the information would be detrimental to the well-being of the child. States Parties shall further ensure that the submission of such a request shall of itself entail no adverse consequences for the person(s) concerned.

4. Lorsque la séparation résulte de mesures prises par un Etat partie, telles que la détention, l'emprisonnement, l'exil, l'expulsion ou la mort (y compris la mort, quelle qu'en soit la cause, survenue en cours de détention) des deux parents ou de l'un d'eux, ou de l'enfant, l'Etat partie donne sur demande aux parents, à l'enfant ou, s'il y a lieu, à un autre membre de la famille les renseignements essentiels sur le lieu où se trouvent le membre ou les membres de la famille, à moins que la divulgation de ces renseignements ne soit préjudiciable au bien-être de l'enfant. Les Etats parties veillent en outre à ce que la présentation d'une telle demande n'entraîne pas en elle-même de conséquences fâcheuses pour la personne ou les personnes intéressées.

PART I

Article 8: The Right to Preservation of Identity

CHAPTER ONE

INTRODUCTION*

1. Article 8 of the Convention on the Rights of the Child concerns the rights of children to identity and their rights to have such identity preserved or, where necessary, re-established by the State.

2. In order to understand the unique nature of Article 8 of the CRC, it is necessary to pay particular attention to the reason for its inclusion in the Convention. The scope of the implementation of Article 8 is very much determined by this historical reason. But the Convention is a living instrument and its interpretation should reflect new developments that may arise in the area of children's rights.

So after having given an overview of comparable human rights provisions (Chapter Two), in Chapter Three I shall present in some detail the drafting history of Article 8, followed by its interpretation in the light of this history. I will conclude with some thoughts about the possible meaning of the right to preserve your identity beyond the particular situation that led to this provision.

---

* January 2005.

CHAPTER TWO

COMPARISON WITH OTHER INTERNATIONAL
HUMAN RIGHTS PROVISIONS

3. Article 8 of the CRC is a unique international human rights provision. There is no other international (or regional) human rights treaty that contains a provision similar to Article 8.

4. The right to be registered immediately after birth (see Article 24 of the CCPR and also Article 7 of the CRC) can be seen as closely related to the rights of every person to her or his own identity. One can also refer to Article 16 of the CCPR concerning the right of everyone to recognition as a person before the law. But none of these articles mentions the identity as such nor do they indicate what important components of a person's identity are. A birth certificate may be an important tool for somebody's identification but the concept of identity goes beyond the (non-)issuance of a birth certificate.

5. Finally it should be noted that the European Court of Human Rights, in its interpretation of Article 8 of the ECHR, in particular the right to respect for private life, has ruled that this right covers an individual's physical and social identity, such as gender identification,[1] name, sexual orientation and sexual life and the right to personal development and personal autonomy.[2]

---

[1] See in this regard the judgement of the Court in Christine Goodwin v. United Kingdom. ECtHR, *Goodwin* v. *United Kingdom*, 11 July 2001, App. No. 289957/95, *Reports* 2002–VI. It concluded that the refusal to recognize in law a change of sex (transsexual) was an unjustified interference in an important aspect of an individual's personal identity.

[2] See ECtHR, *Pretty* v. *United Kingdom*, 29 April 2002, App. No. 2346/02, *Reports* 2002–III, para. 61.

CHAPTER THREE

THE SCOPE OF ARTICLE 8

1. *Why Article 8 of the CRC?*

6. Between 1975 and 1983, 145 to 170 children disappeared in Argentina during the military junta. They were either kidnapped with their parents by the authorities or they were born to imprisoned women and then separated from their mothers. In 1987, 41 of these children had been located as the result of an intensive search by relatives of the children supported by the then well-known 'Grandmothers of the Plaza Mayo'. Many of these children were adopted, often by adoptive parents working with the militia or police. In the eighties, this kind of politically motivated disappearances of children happened in other countries in the Latin American region like Chile, Guatemala and Peru.[3]

In the light of these experiences, the delegation of Argentina submitted (in 1985 and again in 1986) the draft of a new article to the open-ended working group, which read as follows:

> 'The child has the inalienable right to retain his true and genuine personal, legal and family identity. In the event that a child has been fraudulently deprived of some or all of the elements of his identity, the State must give him special protection and assistance with a view to re-establishing his true and genuine identity as soon as possible. In particular, this obligation of the State includes restoring the child to his blood relations to be brought up.'

7. The proposal generated a lot of discussion. Some delegations were wondering whether the proposed article was necessary because other articles (currently Articles 7, 9, 18 and 21 of the CRC) were already covering the matter of identity (the right to name and nationality in Article 7 of the CRC) and providing for protection in cases of deprivation of parental care and adoption (Articles 9, 18 and 21 of the CRC).

---

[3] See for more information *e.g. The International Children's Rights Monitor* (Defence for Children International, Geneva), Vol. 1, No. 1 and 4 and Vol. 2, No. 1.

Others observed that the concept of 'family identity' was unknown in their laws. A working party was formed to review the proposal and submit a revised text. This text read as follows:

> '1. The States Parties undertake to respect the right of the child to preserve his or her family identity without unlawful interference.
>
> 2. Where a child is illegally separated or removed from his or her lawful custodians or otherwise fraudulently or illegally deprived of some or all elements of this identity, the States shall provide special assistance and protection with a view to re-establishing his or her rightful family identity.'

8. In further discussions the delegations agreed on deleting 'family' and explained the concept of the child's identity by including a non-exhaustive reference to some important elements of that identity: nationality, name and family relations. In the proposed paragraph 2, the part on the separation or removal from his or her lawful custodians was deleted, most likely because that matter is covered in (now) Article 9 of the CRC. Finally, the text of Article 8 as it is, was adopted by the Working Group at its second reading in 1989.[4]

2. The Meaning of Article 8 of the CRC

2.1 The Core Meaning

9. In the light of the history of Article 8 of the CRC, as summarized in the previous paragraph, its core meaning is quite clear and simple: to create a legal basis for the obligation of States Parties to prevent disappearances of children, particularly in politically oppressive situations, and to provide assistance and protection in case such a disappearance occurs with a view to return the child to her/his parents/family. This return should, as far as necessary, come with re-establishing for the child her/his original nationality, name and family relations. The obligation to do this speedily, implicitly refers to the fact that (the passage of) time is a crucial factor. The more time has passed, the more difficult it may become to re-establish (not only on paper but also *de facto*) the original family relations. Respect for the family life which the child *de facto* has (perhaps since birth), may mean that it

---

[4] See for more information about the discussions in the Working Group, S. Detrick (ed.), *A Guide to the 'Travaux Préparatoires'* (Dordrecht, Boston, London, Martinus Nijhoff Publishers, 1992), pp. 291–296.

is not in the best interests of the child to be returned to a family s/he does not know at all. But the term 'speedily' also implies that a State Party is under the obligation to provide immediately the appropriate assistance and protection. 'Appropriate' means all assistance necessary[5] to trace, locate and return the child. If that has been successful, 'appropriate assistance and protection' also includes the provision of support, *e.g.* in terms of counselling and therapy to help the child and her/his family of origin to re-establish *de facto* their family relations.

10. In order to avoid misunderstandings and with reference to the discussion in the Working Group that drafted the Convention, Article 8 of the CRC is:

– <u>not</u> about international child abduction (often in the slipstream of a divorce) which should be combated *inter alia* via bilateral or multilateral agreements;[6]
– <u>not</u> about deprivation of a name and/or nationality and/or family relations via a domestic or inter-country adoption which takes place in accordance with the standards set in Article 21 of the CRC. If that is not the case, the adoption is illegal and the consequences are the result of fraudulent acts and should be void and/or nullifiable. The parents or other family members are in such cases entitled to appropriate assistance and support, to be provided by the State, in their efforts to locate the child and bring her/him back to his family;
– <u>not</u> about the separation from parents (see Articles 9 and 10 of the CRC) or the deprivation of family environment (see Article 20 of the CRC) which may be the result of internal or cross-border displacement (see Article 22 of the CRC). Those situations of separation or deprivation require various actions to be undertaken by the States Parties as spelled out in the Articles mentioned and they focus *inter alia* on reunification of the child with her/his parents/family. The separation and deprivation dealt with in the Articles 9, 10, 20 and 22 of the CRC do not necessarily entail deprivation of the identity of the child, although it may affect in particular her/his family relations. So there may be some overlap with Article 8 of

---

[5] The first proposal used the term 'necessary'; in the revised version it was replaced by 'special'. It is not clear why it was replaced by 'appropriate' but it seems appropriate to assume that 'necessary' actions are also 'appropriate'.

[6] See M. Ely, 'Article 11', in: A. Alen, J. Vande Lanotte, E. Verhellen, F. Ang, E. Berghmans and M. Verheyde (eds.), *A Commentary on the United Nations Convention on the Rights of the Child* (Leiden, Martinus Nijhoff Publishers), forthcoming, and see also the Hague Convention on the Civil Aspect of International Child Abduction (1980).

the CRC, but that overlap can be reduced or even avoided if we stick to the core meaning of Article 8;
- <u>not</u> about the right to a name or nationality, which is covered in Article 7 of the CRC.[7]

11. Finally, it may be said that the drafters of the Convention have based the obligation of a State Party to prevent, combat and remedy (illegal) disappearances of children on respect for the right of the child to preserve her/his identity. Judging with hindsight, one may wonder whether that was necessary, the more so as it has introduced the concept of identity not found in other human rights treaties.

12. The meaning of this concept may be clarified with reference to the drafting history (*travaux préparatoires*) as was done above in explaining what the core meaning of Article 8 of the CRC is. But that drafting history is not decisive for the interpretation of Article 8. I concur with the European Court of Human Rights that has repeatedly stated that the interpretation of the European Convention on Human Rights must be dynamic in the sense that it must be interpreted in the light of developments in social and political attitudes. Its effects cannot be confined to the conceptions of the period when it was drafted or entered into force.[8] The Convention must be interpreted in the light of the present-day conditions.[9]

In other words, some observations on the possible meaning of the preservation of identity seem to be appropriate.

2.2   *The Right to Preserve Your Identity*

13. The Convention does not define identity and one could doubt whether such definition is possible. Erikson defines identity as the subjective feeling of continuously being the same person[10] and there seems to be a consensus that identity is a concept that develops in the course of the child's

---

[7] I. Ziemele, 'Article 7', in: A. Alen, J. Vande Lanotte, E. Verhellen, F. Ang, E. Berghmans and M. Verheyde (eds.), *A Commentary on the United Nations Convention on the Rights of the Child* (Leiden, Martinus Nijhoff Publishers), forthcoming.

[8] *E.g.* ECtHR, *Wemhoff* v. *Germany*, 27 June 1968, *Publications of the Court*, Series A, No. 7, para. 8: it is necessary 'to seek the interpretation that is most appropriate in order to realize the aim and achieve the object of the treaty, not that which would restrict to the greatest possible degree the obligation undertaken by the Parties'.

[9] See *inter alia* ECtHR, *Johnston* v. *Ireland*, 18 December 1986, *Publications of the Court*, Series A, No. 112.

[10] See *e.g.* E. Erikson, *Identity, youth and crisis* (New York, Norton, 1968).

development and that there are different age-related stages in that development. It goes beyond the scope of this commentary to elaborate in detail the (psychological) concept of identity.[11]

14. Article 8 of the CRC limits itself to a non-exhaustive list of elements of the child's identity. The problem of that list is that other articles of the Convention already protect those elements.[12] But what could be other elements of a child's identity? This brings me to the present-day conditions relevant to the child's identity, more in particular the practice of medically assisted procreation.

15. This kind of procreation generates a lot of ethical and legal questions.[13] From the legal perspective, there is *inter alia* a conflict of interests. On the one hand the adults, that is the donor and the (future) parents, want to keep the artificial procreation secret, often with a reference to the right to respect for their privacy (private life). On the other hand, there is the right of the child to information about her/his (biological) origins.

16. In this regard, it is important to note the development in the area of adoption. For a long time, adoption was dealt with in secrecy and anonymity to avoid possible social problems. But nowadays there is broad consensus among the experts that openness facilitates the development of identity, because it gives the possibility of integrating the factual circumstances of life. The concealment of reality – and that applies also to medically assisted procreation – may have serious negative consequences for the development of personal identity and well-being. For parents of a child conceived with medical assistance, it is important to inform the child at the appropriate time. This is in line with their responsibility for the upbringing and <u>development</u> of their child, in which the best interest of the child is their basis concern (Article 18(1) of the CRC).

17. It is, in my opinion, not acceptable and not feasible for a State to force parents by law to provide this information to the child. Not acceptable, because it would result in a disproportionate (and thus an injustice) interference in the family and privacy of both the parents and the child. Not

---

[11] See for an overview of the various theories regarding the development of an identity *e.g.* R. E. Muuss and E. Velder, *Theories of Adolescence* (New York, Random House, 1968), 426 p.

[12] *Cf. supra* No. 10.

[13] See *e.g.* D. Evans (ed.), *Creating the Child. The Ethics, Law and Practice of Assisted Procreation* (The Hague, Kluwer Law International, 1996).

feasible, because it is not possible to *e.g.* set a date/an age before which the child should be informed.

But States Parties to the Convention could and should inform the parents about the importance of openness, both in case of adoption and in case of medically assisted procreation, and actively promote that openness.

18. Given the consensus that openness is in the interest of the child, the next question is whether this openness entails all information about the donor including the personal information like name, date of birth *etc.* There is a small but growing number of States Parties to the CRC that have enacted legislation which gives the child the right to receive personal information about the donor when s/he has reached a specified age (*e.g.* 16 or 18 years) or is mature enough.

19. So far the UN Committee on the Rights of the Child has paid limited attention to Article 8 and its (potential) meaning for the rights of children conceived with medical assistance.[14]

But in the light of the present day developments and a dynamic interpretation of the CRC, it can be considered to include in the right to preserve your identity, the right to be informed about your (biological) origins. At the same time, it is a matter of respect for the rights of donors to protect them from any legal or financial responsibility for the child conceived with their assistance.

20. The matter of donor anonymity is a very much (and quite hotly) debated topic. Medical professionals tend to be more in favour of anonymity whereas lawyers support the full openness as a right of the person artificially conceived.

John Eekelaar rightly posed the question: Would anyone choose to live his or her entire life on the basis that he or she has been deliberately deceived about their genetic origin?[15]

---

[14] See E. Blyth and A. Farnand, 'Anonymity in donor assisted conception and the UN Convention on the Rights of the Child', *The International Journal of Children's Rights*, Vol. 12, No. 2, 2004, pp. 89–104.

[15] As cited by M. Freeman, 'The Rights of the Artificially Procreated Child, Chapter 10' in *The Moral Status of Children. Essays on the Rights of the Child* (The Hague, Kluwer Law International, 1997), p. 199.

21. Finally and even within the 'dynamic' interpretation suggested, one should keep in mind:

- <u>first</u> that Article 8(1) of the CRC contains an important and limiting qualification 'as recognized by law'. It is not fully clear whether this clause should be linked to 'identity' or (only) to family relations.[16]

The clause was first introduced in relation to the term 'family identity' and apparently was meant to address the problem that 'family identity' was an unknown concept in most national legislation.[17] In the light of this history it seems to be arguable that in the current text 'as recognized by law' should be linked to 'family relations'. This may have a particular importance in cases of medically assisted procreation. It means that States Parties may <u>not</u> recognize a family relation between the donor and the child and that is in fact the rule in many if not all States Parties;

- <u>second</u> that para 2 of Article 8 of the CRC has not been written with artificial procreation in mind. But the obligation to respect the right of the child to preserve her or his identity, requires the State Party to undertake all legislative, administrative or other measures (Article 4 of the CRC) to implement that right, interpreting it in a dynamic manner and with the present day conditions in mind.

---

[16] See S. Detrick, *A Commentary on the United Nations Convention on the Rights of the Child* (The Hague, Kluwer Law International, 1999), p. 165.
[17] See S. Detrick, *A Guide to the 'Travaux Préparatoires'*, *o.c.* (note 4), p. 293.

PART II

Article 9: The Right Not to Be Separated from His or Her Parents

CHAPTER ONE

COMPARISON WITH RELATED INTERNATIONAL
HUMAN RIGHTS PROVISIONS*

1. There is no other international human rights treaty that explicitly deals with the matter of separation of children from their parents with an exception for the African Charter on the Rights and Welfare of the Child (hereafter: the African Charter). Article 19 of that Charter is to a significant degree, similar to Article 9 of the CRC. But there are some remarkable differences. To facilitate the comparison the text of Article 19 of the African Charter is as follows:

Article 19: Parent Care and Protection

1. Every child shall be entitled to the enjoyment of parental care and protection and shall, whenever possible, have the right to reside with his or her parents. No child shall be separated from his parents against his will, except when a judicial authority determines in accordance with the appropriate law, that such separation is in the best interest of the child.
2. Every child who is separated from one or both parents shall have the right to maintain personal relations and direct contact with both parents on a regular basis.
3. Where separation results from the action of a State Party, the State Party shall provide the child, or if appropriate, another member of the family with essential information concerning the whereabouts of the absent member or members of the family. States Parties shall also ensure that the submission of such a request shall not entail any adverse consequences for the person or persons in whose respect it is made.
4. Where a child is apprehended by a State Party, his parents or guardians shall, as soon as possible, be notified of such apprehension by that State Party.

Without going into details the following should be noted:

a. the Charter does not require that the determination by a competent authority – as meant in paragraph 1 – is subject to judicial review. It

---

* August 2005.

means that the possibility of an appeal from a separation decision is left to national laws. Furthermore, the African Charter seems to be weaker in the formulation of the criterion 'A separation has to be "in the best interest of the child"' whereas Article 9 adds the qualification 'necessary'. In other words: separation has to be a necessity. This approach is in my opinion more conducive for the realization of the rights and welfare of the child. Given the provision in paragraph 2 of Article 1 of the African Charter (= similar to Article 41 of the CRC) it means that the CRC prevails. This is also applicable to the 'judicial review' provision.

b. the participation of 'all interested parties' (and that is not necessarily limited to child and parents) provided for in paragraph 2 of Article 9 of the CRC is missing from Article 19 of the African Charter. The reason for this omission is unknown (to me). But again the CRC may prevail (see under a).

c. the right of the child to have personal direct and regular contact with her/his parents is provided for in both instruments. That contact can only be refused if it is <u>contrary</u> to the best interests of the child (Article 9(3) of the CRC), but that is not mentioned in the African Charter. It is an important difference because the CRC is apparently based on the assumption that the contact with the parent(s) is in the best interest of the child. The African Charter does not explicitly express that assumption.

d. in paragraph 4 of Article 19, the African Charter has an important provision for the realization of contact between a child deprived of liberty and her/his parents. The right to such contact is explicitly provided for in Article 37(c) of the CRC. But the CRC does (unfortunately) not contain a provision similar to Article 19(4) of the African Charter, although the Havana Rules do recommend in paragraph 22 immediate information to parents.[1]

2. Finally, there are some provisions in other international human rights instruments which are more indirectly relevant to the separation of a child from her/his parents and the maintenance of contact in case of such a separation.

Article 24 of the International Covenant on Civil and Political Rights (hereafter: CCPR) deals with the right of the child to special measures of protection.

---

[1] Havana Rules: UN Rules for the Protection of Juveniles Deprived of their Liberty (UN Doc. A.45/49, 1990), para. 22: 'The information on admission, place, transfer and release should be provided without delay to the parents and guardians or closest relative of the juvenile concerned'.

Such measures include that a child may be separated from his family when circumstances so require.[2] A similar right to special measures of protection is contained in Article 19 of the American Convention on Human Rights and in Article 16 of the Additional Protocol to that Convention.[3] In that article emphasis is on the child of a young age who 'ought not to be separated from his mother', same in exceptional, judicially recognized circumstances.

Article 8 of the European Convention on Human Rights (hereafter: ECHR) contains *inter alia* the right to respect for family life. This right is violated if a child is separated from her/his parents. But that violation can be justified if it meets the conditions set in paragraph 2 of Article 8 of the ECHR. There are quite a number of decisions of the European Court of Human Rights (hereafter: ECtHR) concerning the separation of a child from her/his parents and the interpretation of Article 8 of the ECHR (*Cf. infra*).

---

[2] See Human Rights Committee, *General Comment No. 17: Rights of the child (Art. 24)* (UN Doc. HRI/GEN/1/Rev.7; 12 May 2004), p. 145, para. 6.

[3] Additional Protocol of San Salvador to the American Convention on Human Rights in the Area of Economic, Social and Cultural Rights – 'Protocol of San Salvador', adopted on 17 November 1988, entered into force 16 November 1999.

CHAPTER TWO

THE SCOPE OF ARTICLE 9 OF THE CRC

1. *Introduction*

3. Non-separation of parents and children is the starting point of Article 9 and a principle that States Parties have to uphold, that is: to ensure and protect. Despite this starting point most of the Article is not about the non-separation but about the conditions under which a separation can be justifiable (para. 1), some rules of procedure (para. 2) and provisions meant to maintain the contact between a child and her/his parent(s) in case of separation (paras. 3 and 4). These various aspects of Article 9 will be used to structure the observations and comments concerning the content of this Article. But before doing so, another general remark should be made concerning the relation between Article 9 and Article 10 that makes an explicit reference to Article 9(1). During the drafting of the CRC the chairman of the open-ended Working Group made the following statement about Articles 9 and 10: 'It is the understanding of the Working Group that Article 9 of this Convention is intended to apply to separations that arise in domestic situations, whereas Article 10 is intended to apply to separations involving different countries and relating to cases of family reunification. Article 10 is not intended to affect the general right of States to establish and regulate their respective immigration laws in accordance with their international obligations'.[4]

2. *Non-Separation*

4. The States Parties' obligation 'shall ensure' implies that they have to take positive measures to prevent a separation of a child from her or his parents 'against their will'. The interpretation of this qualification is not completely clear. From the drafting history it is clear that it refers to the will of parents[5] but it can equally refer to the will of both the parents and the

---

[4] S. Detrick, *A Commentary on the United Nations Convention on the Rights of the Child* (The Hague/Boston/London, Martinus Nijhoff Publishers, 1999), p. 170.

[5] S. Detrick (ed.), *The United Nations Convention on the Rights of the Child: A Guide to the 'Travaux Préparatoires'* (Dordrecht, Boston, London, Martinus Nijhoff Publishers, 1992), p. 168, para. 21.

child. The text does not seem to cover a separation against the will of the child alone. Nevertheless the question should be whether the State Party has an obligation regarding this kind of separation, *e.g.* in case the parents agree that their child should be placed in an institution. Some observations:

First: the text initially adopted by the Working Group was 'The State Parties shall ensure that a child shall not be involuntarily separated from his parents'. 'Involuntarily' applies apparently to either the parents <u>and</u> the child or to one of them. The replacement of the term 'involuntarily' with 'against their will' was not explained. But there was also no indication that it was meant to be a substantive change.[6]

Second: it was an assumption of the Working Group and a rather generally accepted principle that parents have the right to specify the place of the child's residence. But it was also proposed that if the place of residence determined by the parents endangers the child's well being, his residence will be decided by a competent State organ. The proposal was ultimately not adopted because it concerns the rights of parents and had no place in such a convention (dealing with State obligations).[7]

Third: during the drafting it was proposed to add to the examples of situations in which separation may be necessary <u>and</u> subject to a determination by a competent authority 'where there is a disagreement between parent(s) and child as to the child's place of residence'. This proposal was withdrawn because the drafters should not attempt to make an exhaustive list of possible reasons for a separation.[8]

On the basis of these observations it can be concluded that States Parties should provide for an adequate remedy for the child in case he or she is – as the result of a decision of her/his parents – separated from her/his parents against her/his will. One could think of providing the possibility of a mediation and if necessary the initiation of a court procedure by the child or her/his legal representative (*e.g.* guardian ad litem) to determine whether that separation is indeed necessary in the best interest of that child.

5. In relation to the States Parties' obligation to ensure non-separation, the UN Committee on the Rights of the Child (hereafter: the CRC Committee) has regularly recommended specific measures to prevent the abandonment

---

[6] *Ibid.*, p. 163, para. 65 and p. 168, para. 21.
[7] *Ibid.*, p. 163, paras. 62, 63 and p. 164, paras. 67–68.
[8] *Ibid.*, p. 168, para. 20.

of children by their parents. This abandonment is often the result of seri-ous economic problems parents are facing. States Parties should therefore, in the opinion of the CRC Committee, provide for *e.g.* family support/allowances in particular for the most vulnerable group of single-parent families.[9]

Non-separation is a particularly difficult problem in case a parent is impris-oned. Some States Parties allow very young children to stay with their mother in prison. Sometimes the length of this stay is limited to one or two years. Generally speaking and given the often very poor living conditions it is very unlikely that such a stay in prison is in the best interest of the child. The CRC Committee has recommended States Parties to take the nec-essary measures to establish alternatives for this form of institutionalisa-tion. At the same time, the States Parties have to create effective opportunities for the child to maintain direct contact with her/his imprisoned parent. There is a growing interest for this dilemma: separate in particular the (very) young children from their parents because they are in prison or not, knowing that a prison does not provide an appropriate environment for babies and young children. A full discussion of this problem goes beyond the scope of this commentary (*Cf. infra* No. 12).

6. One of the most complicated cases of (possible forced) separation occurs in quite a number of States Parties and concerns parents with children who illegally reside in the country. The complication in some of those cases is that parents have lived in the country for a (very) long time, that their child (children) was (were) born there and that ultimately the request for asy-lum or refugee status has been denied. The case of Winata vs. Australia decided by the Human Rights Committee is illustrative for the various aspect of this problem. In this case the Committee observed: 'a decision of the State party to deport two parents and to compel the family to choose whether a 13 years old child, who has attained citizenship of the country after living there for 10 years (the child was born in the country JED), either remains in the State party or accompanies his parents is to be considered interference with the family, at least in circumstances, where, as here, substantial changes

---

[9] *E.g.* CRC Committee, *Concluding Observations: Norway* (UN Doc. CRC/C/15/Add.262, 2005), para. 24: 'take measures to address the causes of the rising number of children who are removed from their families, including through adequate support for biological parents' and *Kyrgyzstan* (UN Doc. CRC/C/15/Add.244, 2004), para. 40: 'Adopt comprehensive strategy and take preventive measures to avoid separation of children from their family environment inter alia by providing parents or guardians with appropriate assistance'.

to long–settled family life would follow in either case. In view of the dura-tion of time, it is incumbent on the State party to demonstrate additional factors justifying the removal of both parents that go beyond a simple enforcement of its immigration laws (. . . .)'.[10]

3. *Separation Necessary in the Best Interest of the Child*

7. Paragraph 1 of Article 9 makes an exception to the right of the child not to be separated from her/his parent under certain conditions and gives some examples of situations in which a separation may be necessary in the best interest of the child. The conditions are the following: necessary for the best interest of the child (3.1), competent authority and subject to judi-cial review (3.2), and participation in the proceedings (3.3).

3.1 *'Necessary for the Best Interests of the Child'*

8. Paragraph 1 (implicitly) requires States Parties to have or introduce law(s) and procedures that are applicable when competent authorities have to determine whether a separation from the parents is necessary for the best interests of the child. Concerning the criteria or factors to be used in this regard the CRC limits itself to two examples of cases in which such sepa-ration may be necessary: cases involving abuse and neglect by parents and cases in which parents are living separated. From the drafting history it is clear that these examples are just illustrations and not an exhaustive list of the possibilities to separate a child from her/his parents. The phrase "such as" in both para. 1 and para. 2 of Article 9 indicate that it is a lim-ited list of examples.[11] It is left to the States Parties to provide in their national child protection acts or similar legislative measures the criteria for a separation necessary for the best interest of the child.

In the implementation of these criteria the State Party is under the obligation to avoid any form of discrimination (Article 2 of the CRC). The separation of a child from her/his parents is an interference not only with the primary

---

[10] Human Rights Committee, *Communication 930/2000 of 26 July 2001: Winata v. Australia* (Annual Report 2001, 199), with some strong dissenting opinions.

[11] See *e.g. Recommendation 1469 (2000)* of the Parliamentary Assembly of the Council of Europe on Mothers and Babies in Prison and the report with the same title of the Social Health and Family Affairs (Committee Doc. 8762, 9 June 2000). See also R. Wolleswinkel, 'Children of Imprisoned Mothers', in: J. C. Willems (ed.), *Developmental and Autonomy Rights of Children* (Antwerp/Oxford/New York, Intersentia, 2002), pp. 191–207.

and common responsibility of the parents for the upbringing and development of their child (Article 18 of the CRC), but also with the right of the child to respect for her/his family life. This family life should be protected by law against arbitrary or unlawful interference (Article 16 of the CRC). The review of the States Parties' reports by the CRC Committee (Articles 43–45 of the CRC) has so far not resulted in a clear picture of the practice of separation under Article 9. One may argue that such picture may never arise from these reports given the differences that exist among States Parties and their margin of appreciation when assessing the best interest of the child. In that regard I like to refer to the European Court of Human Rights, stating that in determining whether an interference in the right to respect for family life is justifiable (Article 8 of the EHCR), it will take into account 'the fact that perceptions as to the appropriateness of intervention by public authorities in the care of children vary from one contracting State to another, depending on such factors as traditions relating to the role of the family and to State intervention in family affairs and the availability of resources for public measures in this area'.[12]

It goes beyond the scope of this commentary to discuss in more details the decisions of the ECtHR that are only binding for the European contracting States under the ECHR. But all those States are at the same time Parties to the CRC and the decisions of the European Court therefore may be considered as guidelines for the interpretation of Article 9 of the CRC.

With reference to the jurisprudence of the ECtHR and acknowledging the regional limitations of that jurisprudence, we may consider the following guidelines as internationally acceptable and in compliance with the object and purpose of the CRC:

– a separation can be considered as necessary in the best interest of the child if there is no other measure available to provide the child with the necessary protection of her/his health and development (physically, mentally and/or otherwise). The State in its intervention is under the obligation to present reasons which sufficiently justify the necessity of the separation;[13]
– a separation should in principle be a temporary measure for the shortest time possible. In other words, a separation decision should not be an infinitive one and should be subject to regular review (Cf. infra No. 10);

---

[12] S. Detrick, *A Guide to the 'Travaux préparatoires'*, o.c. (note 5), p. 170, paras. 26 and 27 and p. 172, paras. 9 and 10.
[13] See for more information *e.g.* U. Kilkelly, *The Child and the European Convention on Human Rights* (Aldershot, Ashgate/Dartmouth, 1999), in particular chapters 8 and 9.

- the decision should be carried out in such a way that reunification with the parent is not unnecessarily impeded;
- but all the above should not exclude the possibility that the best interest of the child demand that the separation from the parents is final.

3.2 'Competent Authority and Subject to Judicial Review'

9. The CRC leaves it to the States Parties to decide whether this authority should be a court or an administrative body. But 'competent' means that the authority specially designated for the determination of the necessity of a separation should not only be mandated to do so ('competent' in legal terms), but also competent in substantive terms. The authority concerned should be well trained and have the necessary knowledge of child psychology and child development, parent-child attachment and of the existing alternative ways and means to address the problems in the parent-child relationship without resorting to a separation.

10. The separation decided by the competent authority should be subject to judicial review. This implies that the law should provide not only for the possibility to appeal from the decision of the court or an administrative body, but also that the decision is not an infinitive one. It means that the decision should be limited in time (*e.g.* for one year) with the possibility to prolong the separation if it is still necessary for the best interest of the child or subject to a periodic review. Compare Article 25 concerning the periodic review of the placement of a child. The separation from the parents by a competent authority is a placement. So even if one would argue that 'judicial review' is limited to an appeal to a higher court or body, Article 25 requires a periodic and substantive review of the necessity of separation.

The right not to be separated implies that the separation should be a measure of last resort for the shortest time possible. This approach can also be found in the jurisprudence of ECtHR. The principle that a separation should be of a temporary nature requires that the State undertakes, promotes and supports efforts to reunify the child with her/his parents if possible and that measures that could negatively affect these efforts, *e.g.* the prohibition of any contact between parent and child, should be avoided.[14] But this does not exclude the possibility that a separation is or becomes final *e.g.* in cases of serious and chronic drug addiction of the parent(s).

---

[14] See *inter alia* ECtHR, *Olsson v. Sweden*, 24 March 1988, Series A., No. 130, and ECtHR, *Johansen v. Norway* 7 August 1996, *Reports*, 1996-III.

3.3   *Participation in the Proceedings*

11. Paragraph 2 of Article 9 is in line with and based on the right to a fair hearing by a competent independent and impartial tribunal (Article 14(1) of the CCPR; see also *inter alia* Article 6 of the ECHR) and on the right of the child to be heard (Article 12, in particular para. 2 of the CRC). 'All interested parties' are obviously the parents and the child, but is not necessarily limited to them. For instance, grandparents can under special circumstances be considered as interested parties and may express as their view that – if a separation is necessary – the child should be placed in their care. The opportunity to participate and make their views known presupposes that the interested parties received all the relevant information *e.g.* reports of social workers and/or psychologists with assessments of the situation that may support the separation. A genuine participation is not possible if information is withheld from the interested parties. This applies equally to parents and children. If the child is too young to understand the information, a representative or an appropriate body can 'translate' it for the child. For more information on the child's right to participate see the commentary to Article 12 of the CRC.[15] Even when a separation is immediately necessary for the protection of the child's physical health (*e.g.* cases of physical or sexual abuse) the State should provide for a hearing, either before the decision is made or if that creates serious risk for further harm for the child, as soon as possible – *e.g.* within 24 hours – after the separation took place.[16] Finally, the proceedings concerned can and most likely will be behind closed doors. This is possible on the basis of Article 14(1) of the CCPR and in line with the child's right to have her/his privacy protected (Article 16 of the CRC).

1.   *Direct and Regular Contact*

12. Paragraph 3 of Article 9 requires the State Party to respect the right of the child separated from her/his parent(s) to maintain personal relations and direct contact with both parents on a regular base. Some remarks:

---

[15] The ECtHR considers this participation of children an integral part of the respect for family life (Article 8 of the ECHR) and of a fair hearing (Article 6 of the ECHR). See *e.g.* the decision of the Court of 27 April 2000, in which the views of 8 year old children played an important role (ECtHR, *L. v. Finland*, 27 April 2000, *Reports* 2000, paras. 126–128).

[16] Compare ECtHR, *Venema v. the Netherlands*, 17 December 2002, *Reports* 2002, in particular paras. 93 and 96.

In the traditional interpretation the obligation of a State Party 'to respect' a right means that the State should not violate the right in question.[17] But the content of paragraph 3 should be read and interpreted in the light of Article 2(1) of the CRC: 'States Parties shall respect and ensure the rights set forth in the present Convention to each child . . . (etc.)' and Article 4 of the CRC 'States Parties shall undertake all appropriate (. . . .) measures for the implementation of the rights recognized in the present Convention . . . (etc.)'. This means that the legal obligation of a State Party is both negative and positive in nature. A State Party must refrain from violation of the right of the child to contact with both parents as described in paragraph 3 of Article 9 (negative obligation). But the positive obligations on States Parties will only be fully discharged 'if individuals are protected by the State, not just against violations of (. . .) rights by its agents, but also against acts committed by private persons or entities that would impart the enjoyment of (. . . .) rights . . . .'.[18]

For the right of the child to maintain direct contact with both parents this means *inter alia* (*e.g.*)

- that a State Party should provide for adequate opportunities for a child to maintain direct contact on a regular basis with the imprisoned parent. The best interest of the child, the seriousness of the crime committed by the parent and the (related) need to apply a strict regime are factors that can play a role in determining the frequency and/or duration of such contact;[19]
- that the decision to place a child in an institution should be implemented in such a way that he/she can maintain direct and regular contact with her/his parents. This may imply avoiding a placement (too) far away from the parental home or a placement of two or more children of the same parents in two or more different institutions;[20]

---

[17] See *e.g.* T. Buergenthal, 'To Respect and Ensure: State Obligations and Permissible Derogations', in: L. Henkin (ed.), *The International Bill of Rights; The Covenant on Civil and Political Rights* (New York, Columbia University Press, 1981), pp. 72–91.

[18] See Human Rights Committee, *General Comment No. 31: The Nature of the General Legal Obligation Imposed on States Parties to the Covenant* (UN Doc. CCPR/C/21/Rev.1/Add.13, 2004).

[19] See *e.g.* ECtHR, *Messina v. Italy*, 28 September 2000, *Reports* 2000-X, paras. 70 and 73.

[20] Compare *e.g.* ECtHR, *Olsson v. Sweden*, 24 March 1988, Series A, No. 130 (1989): children dispersed over some distance and ECtHR, *Covezzi and Morselli v. Italy*, Decision of 24 January 2002: four children placed in different locations.

– that the State Party should undertake efforts to enable or to facilitate the contact of the child with her/his parent(s).[21] This may include the support for or establishment of mediation or other support services in case the realization of the contact meets practical and/or emotional problems on the part of one of the involved persons.[22]

13. For all of the above and other situations the key and decisive criterion is the best interests of the child. One should take note of the (implicit) assumption that (in general) contact between the child and her/his parent(s) is in her/his best interests. Contact can only be denied if it is contrary (= in conflict with) the best interests of the child. The unilateral opposition of one of the parents, cannot, in the opinion of the Committee be considered an exceptional circumstance which could justify non-maintenance of personal relations and direct and regular between the child and both parents.[23]

It should also be noted that the views of the child have to be taken into account and given due weight in accordance with the age and maturity of the child (Article 12 of the CRC) (*Cf. supra*: the comments under No. 11 regarding involvement in the proceedings). The approach of paragraph 3 – the contact as a right of the child – means that the views of the child should play an important role. If the child is capable of expressing her/his views and if he/she has the well founded opinion that he/she does not want to maintain contact with the parent, the respect for her/his right entails that a contact he/she does not want should not be imposed/enforced.

14. Finally, the way paragraph 3 is phrased it suggests that there is a difference between personal relations and direct and regular contact. From the drafting history it is not clear why direct and regular contact was added. One could argue that in order to maintain personal relations, it is necessary to have direct and regular contact. But it should not mean that in case this direct and regular contact is practically very limited or impossible (*e.g.* due to geographic distance) personal relations cannot be maintained. Such

---

[21] Compare *e.g.* ECtHR, *Nuutinen v. Finland*, 27 June 2000, 34 EHRR 358 (2002), ECtHR, *K and T v. Finland*, 12 July 2001, *Reports* 2001; and ECtHR, *Hokkanen v. Finland*, 23 September 1994, Series A, No. 299-A; 19 EHRR 139 (1995).
[22] Compare in this regard *e.g.* the detailed observations concerning the organization of and support for contact between the child and his parent: ECtHR, *Scozzari and Giunta v. Italy*, 13 July 2000, paras. 173–183.
[23] Communication 201/1985, *Hendriks v. The Netherlands*, 27 July 1988, para. 10.4 (Annual report 1988, 230).

relations can also be developed and maintained via correspondence, email, telephone etc. Legislative measures could *e.g.* include a provision explicitly containing the right of the child to use such means for maintaining personal relations with her/his parent(s); think for instance of a parent imprisoned in a far away prison. Correspondence in that situation is also protected under Article 16 of the CRC against arbitrary and unlawful interferences. It means that a State Party should have strong and convincing arguments to open letters of a child to her/his imprisoned parent(s).

5. *Information Concerning the Whereabouts*

15. In case the separation of a child from her or his parents is the result of an action by the State Party – and paragraph 4 gives some examples of such actions – essential information concerning the whereabouts of the absent child or parent should be provided to the parent(s), the child or if appropriate another member of the family. The obligation to provide this information is (unfortunately) limited to cases in which it is requested. I assume that such a request can be made by a child, a parent or another appropriate family member. It is apparently left to the State Party to decide which family member can be considered as appropriate, but one could think of grandparents, brothers/sisters of the child or an aunt or uncle.

It would have been more conducive for the realization of the right of the child enshrined in paragraph 3 if the State Party had been obliged to provide this information as soon as possible, that is as soon as the authorities know the whereabouts of the parent(s) or the child. It should be noted that Article 19 of the African Charter (*Cf. supra* No. 1) requires a State Party to notify the parents or guardians as soon as possible if the child is arrested and placed in custody. A similar provision can be found in Rule 10.1 of the Beijing Rules. In the light of Article 41 of the CRC, the African States Parties to the CRC, which are also a State Party to the African Charter, should not wait for a request before informing the parents concerning the whereabouts of their apprehended child.

Given the purpose of the provision in paragraph 4 'essential information' includes at the least specific information about the address of the parent's or child's location and about the possibilities to visit the parent or child. In this regard it should be noted that Article 37(c) of the CRC gives every child deprived of liberty the right to maintain contact with her/his family through <u>correspondence</u> and <u>visits</u>.

It is hard to imagine why or when the provision of information as meant in paragraph 4 would be detrimental for the well being of the child. For instance: even if a parent has died while in the custody of the State, I don't see why it would be detrimental for the well being of the child to inform her/him about this fact. If the child is too young to understand this information, it could be given to the other parent or an appropriate family member and left to their discretion to decide when that child is mature enough to receive that information.

Finally and because the information should be provided upon request, the State Party has to ensure that the submission of such a request shall not entail adverse consequences for the person(s) concerned.